50 Eggcellent Egg-Free Breakfast Recipes

Because People with Egg Allergies Deserve a Good Breakfast, Too!

By Randi Lynn Millward

PublishAmerica
Baltimore

First printing

PublishAmerica has allowed this work to remain exactly as the author intended, verbatim, without editorial input.

This publication contains the opinions and ideas of its author. Author intends to offer information of a general nature. Neither the author nor the publisher are engaged in rendering medical, health or any other kind of personal professional services to the reader. The reader should consult his or her own physician before relying on any information set forth in or implied from this publication. Any reliance on the information herein is at the reader's own discretion.

The author and publisher specifically disclaim all responsibility for any liability, loss, or right, personal or otherwise, which is incurred as a consequence, directly or indirectly, of the use and application of any contents of this book. They further make no representations or warranties with respect to the accuracy or completeness of the contents of this work and specifically disclaim all warranties including without limitation any implied warranty of fitness for a particular purpose. Any recommendations are made without any guarantee on the part of the author or the publisher.

Hardcover 978-1-4489-1687-0
Softcover 978-1-60749-988-6
PUBLISHED BY PUBLISHAMERICA, LLLP
www.publishamerica.com
Baltimore

Printed in the United States of America

Dedication

To my daughter, Aurora, my inspiration, and to God my Creator.

Table of Contents

Introduction

In our culture, breakfast generally centers around eggs—omelets, scrambled eggs, eggs benedict. If eggs aren't at the center of the meal, they're almost always at least an ingredient in the dish—pancakes, French toast, muffins. A person with egg allergies might just resign himself to cold cereal for breakfast everyday. After all, an allergic reaction would at best cause an itchy rash, and at worst be life-threatening.

Breakfast doesn't have to consist of only cold cereal though. I've created an abundance of egg-free breakfast recipes that range from light to hearty, from healthy to indulgent. Most of them are very similar to what allergy-free people eat for breakfast. After all, people with egg allergies deserve a good breakfast, too.

The recipes require no "powdered egg substitute." They're not laden with artificial ingredients. They're recipes that I myself use, and I have pretty high standards regarding what my family eats.

When my youngest daughter began trying solid food as a baby, she had numerous reactions. She had problems with milk, strawberries, and even apricots. The only major intolerance or allergy that hung on, though, was her egg allergy.

It was immensely difficult protecting her from eggs. They seemed to be everywhere. Finally, I just got rid of every food in my house that could cause her to have an allergic reaction. I called ahead to restaurants to ask if there would be anything there that she could eat, and I brought food for her from home if I wasn't absolutely sure that she wouldn't be served something that was tainted with eggs.

My husband didn't have the dedication that I did, though. He complained that I never made him scrambled eggs or pancakes anymore. He hated that there were no eggs in the house. I didn't want to make those things for him because if my daughter saw him eating them, she'd want some, too, and it not only broke my heart to have to tell her that she couldn't have any because the eggs in them would hurt her, but I also feared that my husband would give her some since he has always been oblivious to ingredients, allergens, and potential allergens in foods.

Finally, I decided to get creative. If my husband wanted pancakes, I would make him pancakes, but I would find a way for my daughter to be able to eat them, too. I bought many allergy cookbooks, but they all seemed to be for people with multiple food allergies. I couldn't find one for people who were only allergic to eggs. That's when I came up with the recipes in this book. I tried some recipes that failed miserably. I tweaked some recipes. I gave up on others. Then, finally, I had my collection of egg-free breakfast recipes that my whole family could enjoy.

Some of the recipes would normally contain eggs. Others are naturally egg-free. All of them are a great alternative to cold cereal.

The recipes themselves may be safe, but be careful of the ingredients you use with the recipes contained in this book. Always check food labels for allergens listed. Just because an allergen isn't an ingredient in the product doesn't mean that the food is safe. Some products are manufactured in a facility that also processes eggs and other known allergens. That means that there's a significant risk of cross-contamination. Egg proteins could potentially be introduced into the other products that are manufactured in the same facility.

Consider no packaged or processed foods safe unless you check all of the ingredients and allergy information on the package. If it's not listed, contact the manufacturer for the information. I personally have seen potential allergens such as eggs, fish, peanuts, tree nuts, soy, and milk on everything from frozen vegetables to teething biscuits, steak sauce to pasta, cereal to canned spinach, and even chocolate. So remember, always check for allergy information.

About the Ingredients

Many of the recipes for baked goods in this cookbook call for milled flaxseed and water. The combination of the two makes for a good substitute for eggs. You could buy whole flaxseeds and grind them in a coffee grinder, but milled flaxseed isn't difficult to find. It's available in the baking aisle of most grocery stores. I buy Hodgson Mill brand milled flaxseed at Wal-Mart.

Some of the recipes in this cookbook call for white flour, some for whole wheat flour. The two can be used interchangeably in most of the recipes in this book, but you may need to adjust the liquid in the recipe.

If you would like to substitute white flour in a recipe that calls for whole wheat flour, either add the liquid ingredients in slowly until reaching the desired consistency and omit the leftover portion, or stir in additional flour 1/8 cup at a time until the desired consistency is reached.

If you would like to substitute whole wheat flour in a recipe that calls for white flour, either add additional liquid 1 tablespoon at a time until the desired consistency is reached, or use ¾ of the amount of flour called for, and slowly add more of the remaining flour until the desired consistency is reached, and omit the leftover portion of whole wheat flour.

About the Equipment

As with all appliances, temperature variances may occur. If your stove, oven, waffle iron, or griddle is cooking the food too fast or too slowly, adjust the temperature accordingly.

The recipes in this cookbook that were cooked on a griddle were tested on a cast iron griddle on a stovetop.

The Recipes

Apple Cinnamon Pancakes

Ingredients:
1 c. whole wheat flour
2 tsp. baking powder
1 tbsp. sugar
¼ tsp. salt
½ tsp. cinnamon
2/3 c. milk
1 tbsp. canola oil
¼ c. applesauce
½ c. peeled, cored, grated apple

Preparation:
1. Preheat a griddle to medium to medium-high heat.

2. In a medium bowl, combine the flour, baking powder, sugar, salt and cinnamon.

3. Stir in the milk, canola oil, applesauce, and grated apple until just combined. Do not overmix.

4. Lightly grease the griddle just before cooking.

5. Drop the batter by ¼ cupfuls onto the griddle, and cook until edges are beginning to dry and bubbles begin to appear on top.

6. Flip the pancakes, and cook them another 1-2 minutes.

7. Serve warm with butter and syrup if desired.

Apple Raisin Waffles

Ingredients:
1 c. whole wheat flour
1 tbsp. baking powder
1 tbsp. sugar
½ tsp. salt
1 tsp. milled flaxseed
1 tsp. cinnamon
¾ c. milk
¼ c. canola oil
¼ c. raisins
½ c. peeled, cored, shredded apple

Preparation:
1. Preheat waffle iron.

2. In a medium bowl, combine the flour, baking powder, sugar, salt, flaxseed, and cinnamon.

3. Stir in the milk, canola oil, raisins, and apple.

4. Lightly spray the waffle iron with nonstick cooking spray.

5. Pour the batter by 1/3 cupfuls into the waffle iron, and close the lid.

6. Cook 2-3 minutes or until the amount of steam emitted by the waffle iron decreases.

7. Remove the waffles from the waffle iron, and serve warm with butter and syrup if desired.

Makes 6-8 four-inch square waffles.

Apple Walnut Oatmeal

Ingredients:
3 c. quick oats
1 1/2 c. water
1 c. applesauce
1 tsp. cinnamon
¼ c. brown sugar
½ c. chopped walnuts

Preparation:
1. In a saucepan on the stove, bring the water to a boil.

2. When the water begins to boil, stir in the oats, applesauce, and cinnamon.

4. Cook for about 1 minute.

5. Stir in the brown sugar and walnuts.

6. Serve warm.

Bacon Breakfast Sandwiches

Ingredients:
4 English muffins, bagels, or biscuits
8 strips of bacon
8 oz. firm tofu
4 slices American cheese

Preparation:
1. In a skillet on the stove, fry the bacon until it reaches your desired crispiness.

2. If using English muffins or bagels, split them open, and toast them while the bacon is cooking. If using biscuits, split them open, and set them aside.

3. Remove the bacon from the pan, and drain it on a thin layer of paper towels.

4. Slice the tofu into four 2-ounce slices.

5. In the same pan that you just used to cook the bacon, and without washing the pan afterwards, cook the tofu over low heat for about 1 minute on each side or until just warmed through.

6. To assemble the sandwiches, place a slice of tofu on each of the English muffin, bagel, or biscuit bottoms.

7. Top each slice of tofu with a slice of cheese.

8. Top each slice of cheese with 2 slices of cooked bacon.

9. Place the English muffin, bagel, or biscuit tops on the sandwiches.

10. Serve warm.

Baked Apples

Ingredients:
4 apples, peeled, cored, and halved
8 tsp. butter
1 tsp. cinnamon
¼ c. brown sugar
¼ c. real maple syrup
1 c. granola
1 c. whipped cream

Preparation:
1. Preheat oven to 325 degrees F.

2. Lightly grease a 9x13-inch pan with nonstick cooking spray.

3. Arrange the apples in the pan, core side up.

4. Place 1 teaspoon of butter on each piece of apple.

5. In a separate bowl, stir together the cinnamon, brown sugar, and maple syrup.

6. Drizzle the cinnamon mixture evenly over the apples.

7. Bake the apples for 15 minutes, or until they reach your desired tenderness.

8. Remove the apples from the oven, and allow them to sit for 10 minutes to cool.

9. To serve, top each piece of apple with 1/8 cup of granola and 1/8 cup of whipped cream.

10. Serve warm.

Baked Pears

Ingredients:
4 pears, peeled, cored, and halved
4 tsp. butter
½ c. chopped walnuts
1 tsp. cinnamon
½ tsp. ginger
¼ c. brown sugar
¼ c. real maple syrup
*optional, whipped cream

Preparation:
1. Preheat oven to 325 degrees F.

2. Lightly grease a 9x13-inch pan with nonstick cooking spray.

3. Arrange the pears in the pan, core side up.

4. Place ½ teaspoon of butter on each piece of pear.

5. In a separate bowl, stir together the chopped walnuts, cinnamon, ginger, brown sugar, and maple syrup.

6. Spoon the cinnamon mixture evenly over the pears.

7. Bake the pears for 8-10 minutes, or until they reach your desired tenderness.

8. Remove the pears from the oven, and allow them to sit for 5 minutes to cool.

9. Serve warm, with whipped cream if desired.

Banana Spice Oatmeal

Ingredients:
3 c. quick oats
2 c. water
1 large, over-ripe banana
1 tsp. cinnamon
¼ tsp. ginger
1/8 tsp. nutmeg
¼ c. brown sugar

Preparation:
1. In a saucepan on the stove, bring the water to a boil.

2. While waiting for the water to boil, peel and mash the banana with a fork.

3. When the water begins to boil, stir in the oats, banana, cinnamon, ginger, and nutmeg.

4. Cook for about 1 minute.

5. Stir in the brown sugar.

6. Serve warm.

Berry Bread

Ingredients:
2 c. flour
1 c. sugar
1 tbsp. baking powder
1 tsp. baking soda
½ tsp. salt
2 tbsp. canola oil
1 c. milk
1 c. blueberries
1 c. chopped strawberries
½ c. dried cranberries

Preparation:
1. Preheat oven to 350 degrees F, and grease a loaf pan.

2. In a large bowl, combine the flour, sugar, baking powder, baking soda, and salt.

3. Stir in the canola oil and milk until just combined.

4. Gently fold in the blueberries, strawberries and cranberries.

5. Pour the batter into the prepared pan.

6. Bake 45-55 minutes, or until a toothpick inserted in the center comes out clean.

7. Serve warm or at room temperature.

Blueberry Lemon Yogurt Parfaits

Ingredients:
2 c. lemon yogurt
2 c. blueberries
1 c. granola
1 c. whipped cream

Preparation:
1. Start with four clear 12-ounce milkshake glasses or tall glass dessert dishes.

2. Spoon ¼ cup of blueberries into the bottom of each glass.

3. Top the blueberries with ¼ cup of yogurt.

4. Top the yogurt with another ¼ cup of blueberries.

5. Top the blueberries with another ¼ cup of yogurt.

6. Top the yogurt with ¼ cup of granola.

7. Top the granola with ¼ cup of whipped cream.

8. Serve immediately, or refrigerate and serve cold later.

Blueberry Scones

Ingredients:
2 c. flour
½ c. sugar
1 tbsp. baking powder
¼ tsp. salt
1 tbsp. lemon zest
1/3 c. butter
1 c. blueberries, fresh or frozen
1/3 c. milk

Preparation:
1. Preheat oven to 400 degrees F, and grease a baking sheet.

2. In a medium bowl, combine the flour, sugar, baking powder, and salt.

3. Cut the butter into the dry ingredients with a pastry blender, forks, or knives until crumbly.

4. Stir in the lemon zest and blueberries.

5. Add the milk, and stir until combined.

6. Knead the dough 5-10 times on a lightly floured surface.

7. Pat the dough into a circle with a thickness of about 1 inch.

8. Transfer the dough to the prepared baking sheet, and score the top of it into 8 triangles.

9. Bake for 20 minutes, turning the pan and re-scoring the dough half way through the baking time, or until lightly browned and a toothpick inserted into the center comes out clean.

10. Let the scone cool slightly, then break or cut into 8 triangles.

11. Serve warm or at room temperature, with butter or jelly if desired.

Breakfast Banana Splits

Ingredients:
4 bananas, peeled
2 c. vanilla yogurt
2 tbsp. strawberry jam
½ c. crushed pineapple
4 tsp. chocolate syrup
1 c. whipped cream
½ c. chopped pecans

Preparation:
1. Place each banana in an individual bowl or banana split dish.

2. Top each banana with ½ cup vanilla yogurt, 2 teaspoons strawberry jam, 1/8 cup crushed pineapple, 1 teaspoon chocolate syrup, ¼ cup whipped cream, and 1/8 cup chopped pecans.

3. Serve immediately.

Breakfast Burgers

Ingredients:
4 English muffins
1 lb. ground ham
1 c. shredded cheddar cheese
¼ c. diced onion
¼ c. diced green pepper
½ c. peeled, shredded potato

Preparation:
1. In a large bowl, combine the ground ham, cheddar cheese, onion, green pepper, and potato.

2. Divide the ham mixture into quarters, and shape each quarter into a patty.

3. Fry the patties on the stovetop in a large, ungreased skillet over medium heat for about 5 minutes on each side until cooked through.

4. While the patties are cooking, split the English muffins, and toast them until they're lightly browned.

5. When the patties are cooked, place each one on an English muffin, and top with remaining muffin halves.

6. Serve warm.

Breakfast Pizza

Ingredients:
1 12-inch pre-made, cooked pizza crust
½ c. cream cheese, softened
1 c. bacon bits
1 c. crumbled extra firm tofu
2 c. shredded cheddar cheese

Preparation:
1. Preheat oven to 350 degrees F.

2. Place the pizza crust on a pizza pan.

3. In a small bowl, combine the cream cheese and ½ cup of the cheddar cheese.

4. Spread the cheese mixture evenly on the pizza crust.

5. Sprinkle the bacon bits and tofu on the prepared crust.

6. Top with the remaining 1 ½ cups of shredded cheddar cheese.

7. Bake for 15 minutes, or until cheese just begins to brown.

8. Serve warm.

Buttery Banana Sweet Rolls

Ingredients:
1 loaf frozen bread dough, thawed
2 over-ripe bananas, peeled and thinly sliced
1/3 c. butter, softened
¼ c. brown sugar
1/8 c. white sugar

Preparation:
1. Allow the dough to rise as directed on the package.

2. Grease a 9x13-inch pan.

3. In a small bowl, stir together the butter, brown sugar, and white sugar.

4. Roll the dough out into a 12x9-inch rectangle.

5. Spread the sugar mixture evenly over the dough.

6. Top evenly with banana slices.

7. Roll the dough up jelly roll style into a log.

8. Cut the dough into 12 pieces, and place the pieces swirl side up in the prepared pan.

9. Cover and let rise 40-45 minutes.

10. Preheat the oven to 375 degrees F.

11. Place the rolls in the preheated oven and bake for 20-25 minutes or until light brown.

12. Remove from oven, and turn out onto a serving platter or pan immediately.

13. Scrape any remaining syrup from the bottom of the pan, and drizzle it on top of the rolls.

14. Serve warm or at room temperature.

Cheesy Spinach Tomato Broiled Bagels

Ingredients:
2 whole wheat bagels
½ c. frozen spinach, thawed and drained
½ c. diced tomato
½ c. shredded mozzarella cheese
¼ c. grated parmesan cheese

Preparation:
1. Combine the spinach, tomato, mozzarella, and parmesan.

2. Split the bagels open.

3. Top each bagel with ¼ of the cheese and vegetable mixture.

4. Broil 3-5 minutes or until cheese is melted and beginning to brown.

5. Serve warm.

Chocolate Chip Banana Muffins

Ingredients:
¾ c. mashed banana
1 c. vanilla yogurt
1 tbsp. canola oil
3 tbsp. water
2 tsp. baking soda
1 tbsp. ground flaxseed
3/4 c. sugar
1/8 tsp. salt
2 ½ c. whole wheat flour
½ c. chocolate chips

Preparation:
1. Preheat oven to 400 degrees F.

2. Lightly grease 18 nonstick muffin cups with nonstick cooking spray.

3. In a medium bowl, combine the banana, yogurt, oil, water, soda, sugar, and salt.

4. Add the flour and chocolate chips, and stir until just combined. Don't overmix the batter.

5. Divide the batter evenly between the 18 muffin cups.

6. Bake on the center oven rack for 20 minutes or until lightly browned.

7. Allow the muffins to cool before removing them from the cups.

8. Serve warm or at room temperature.

Cinnamon Nut Sticky Rolls

Ingredients:
1 loaf frozen bread dough, thawed
1/3 c. butter, softened
½ c. sugar
1 tsp. cinnamon
½ c. chopped pecans or walnuts

Preparation:
1. Allow the dough to rise as directed on the package.

2. Grease a 9x13-inch pan.

3. In a small bowl, stir together the butter, sugar, cinnamon, and nuts.

4. Roll the dough out into a 12x9-inch rectangle.

5. Spread the sugar mixture evenly over the dough.

6. Roll the dough up jelly roll style into a log.

7. Cut the dough into 12 pieces, and place the pieces swirl side up in the prepared pan.

8. Cover and let rise 40-45 minutes.

9. Preheat the oven to 375 degrees F.

10. Place the rolls in the preheated oven and bake for 20-25 minutes or until light brown.

11. Remove from oven, and turn out onto a serving platter immediately.

12. Scrape any remaining sticky sugar syrup from the bottom of the pan, and drizzle it on top of the rolls.

13. Serve warm or at room temperature.

Cinnamon Rolls

Ingredients:
1 loaf frozen bread dough, thawed
¼ c. butter, softened
1 c. sugar
2 tsp. cinnamon

Preparation:
1. Allow the dough to rise as directed on the package.

2. Grease a 9x13-inch pan.

3. In a small bowl, stir together the butter, sugar, and cinnamon.

4. Roll the dough out into a 12x9-inch rectangle.

5. Spread the sugar mixture evenly over the dough.

6. Roll the dough up jelly roll style into a log.

7. Cut the dough into 12 pieces, and place the pieces swirl side up in the prepared pan.

8. Cover and let rise 45-50 minutes.

9. Preheat the oven to 350 degrees F.

10. Place the rolls in the preheated oven and bake for 20 minutes or until light brown.

11. Remove from oven, and allow to cool slightly.

12. Serve warm or at room temperature.

Coconut Chocolate Chip Bread

Ingredients:
2 c. flour
1 c. sugar
1 tbsp. baking powder
1 tsp. baking soda
½ tsp. salt
2 tbsp. canola oil
1 c. milk
1 c. chocolate chips
1 c. shredded coconut

Preparation:
1. Preheat oven to 350 degrees F, and grease a loaf pan.

2. In a large bowl, combine the flour, sugar, baking powder, baking soda, and salt.

3. Stir in the canola oil and milk until just combined.

4. Gently fold in the chocolate chips and shredded coconut.

5. Pour the batter into the prepared pan.

6. Bake 45-55 minutes, or until a toothpick inserted in the center comes out clean.

7. Serve warm or at room temperature.

Corned Beef Hash

Ingredients:
1 lb. corned beef, diced
2 c. potatoes, shredded
1 c. diced onion
½ tsp. celery salt
1 tsp. ground black or white pepper
¼ c. butter

Preparation:
1. Melt the butter over low heat in a large skillet on the stove.

2. Add the corned beef, potatoes, onion, celery salt, and ground pepper.

3. Increase the heat to medium-high, and cook the hash for 5-7 minutes, stirring occasionally.

4. Cover the pan, reduce the heat to low, and cook for 3 minutes.

5. Remove the lid, and flip the hash to cook the other side.

5. Replace the lid, and cook for 3 more minutes before removing it from the heat.

6. Serve warm.

Buttery Banana Sweet Rolls

Cranberry Scones

21-month old, egg-allergic Aurora enjoying egg-free gingerbread
with whipped cream on Christmas morning

Peach Coffee Cake

Peanut Butter & Jelly Bars

Peanut Butter & Jelly Pancakes

Pumpkin Muffins

Rice Pudding

Sausage Gravy over Drop Biscuits

Sausage Pinwheels

Waffles

Cranberry Scones

Ingredients:
2 c. flour
½ c. sugar
1 tbsp. baking powder
¼ tsp. salt
1 tbsp. orange zest
1/3 c. butter
½ c. chopped cranberries, fresh, frozen, or dried
1/3 c. milk
*optional, ¼ c. chopped walnuts

Preparation:
1. Preheat oven to 400 degrees F, and grease a baking sheet.

2. In a medium bowl, combine the flour, sugar, baking powder, and salt.

3. Cut the butter into the dry ingredients with a pastry blender, forks, or knives until crumbly.

4. Stir in the orange zest, cranberries, and walnuts.

5. Add the milk, and stir until combined.

6. Knead the dough 5-10 times on a lightly floured surface.

7. Pat the dough into a circle with a thickness of about 1 inch.

8. Transfer the dough to the prepared baking sheet, and score the top of it into 8 triangles.

9. Bake for 20 minutes, turning the pan and re-scoring the dough half way through the baking time, or until lightly browned and a toothpick inserted into the center comes out clean.

10. Let the scone cool slightly, then break or cut into 8 triangles.

11. Serve warm or at room temperature, with butter or jelly if desired.

English Muffin Pizzas

Ingredients:
2 whole wheat English muffins
½ c. tomato sauce
1 c. shredded mozzarella cheese
¼ c. diced, cooked ham
¼ c. diced onion
¼ c. diced green pepper
* optional, ½ c. crumbled tofu

Preparation:
1. Split English muffins apart into two halves.

2. Spread each English muffin with 1/8 cup of tomato sauce.

3. Sprinkle each muffin with 1/8 cup of shredded mozzarella.

4. Sprinkle the ham, onion, green pepper, and tofu, if desired, evenly on top of the cheese.

5. Top each muffin with 1/8 cup of shredded mozzarella.

6. Place the prepared pizzas on an ungreased pan.

7. Broil for 3-5 minutes, or until cheese begins to brown.

8. Serve warm.

Frosted Fruit Salad

Ingredients:
1 c. cream cheese, softened
1 c. whipped cream
1/3 c. honey
1 c. banana slices
2 c. grapes, halved
1. c. chopped, cored apple
½ c. chopped walnuts

Preparation:
1. In a mixing bowl, mix the cream cheese, whipped cream, and honey until well combined.

2. Stir in the bananas, grapes, apple, and walnuts.

3. Serve or refrigerate immediately.

Gingerbread

Ingredients:
2 ½ c. whole wheat flour
½ c. sugar
2 tsp. baking powder
1 tsp. cinnamon
1/4 tsp. ginger
1/4 tsp. nutmeg
1/4 tsp. salt
1 ½ tbsp. milled flaxseed
1 ¼ c. hot water
¼ c. canola oil
¾ c. molasses

Preparation:
1. Preheat oven to 350 degrees F, and grease a 9x9-inch pan with nonstick cooking spray.

2. In a medium bowl, stir together the flour, sugar, baking powder, cinnamon, ginger, nutmeg, salt, and flaxseed.

3. Add the hot water, oil, and molasses to the dry ingredients, and stir until free of lumps.

4. Pour the batter into the prepared pan.

5. Bake for 25 minutes, or until a toothpick inserted in the center comes out clean.

6. Serve warm, at room temperature, or chilled, with whipped cream if desired.

Ham & Cheese Biscuits

Ingredients:
2 c. whole wheat flour
1 tbsp. baking powder
¼ tsp. garlic salt
1 tsp. onion powder
¼ c. butter
¾ c. milk
1 tsp. parsley
½ c. precooked diced ham
½ c. shredded cheddar cheese

Preparation:
1. Preheat oven to 450 degrees F.

2. In a medium bowl, combine the flour, baking powder, garlic salt, and onion powder.

3. Cut the butter into dry ingredients with a pastry mixer, forks, or knives.

4. Stir in the parsley, ham, and cheese.

5. Add the milk, and mix with a fork until a ball forms.

5. Turn the dough onto a lightly floured surface, and knead for 1 minute.

6. Roll the dough out to a ½-inch thickness

7. Slice the dough into 12 pieces with a knife, or cut out desired shapes with a cookie cutter.

8. Place the biscuits on an ungreased cookie sheet, and bake for 10-12 minutes.

9. Serve warm.

Ham & Potato Breakfast Casserole

Ingredients:
2-lb. package frozen hash brown potatoes
½ c. diced onion
2 c. cubed ham
1 c. sour cream
1 c. chicken broth
2 tbsp. flour
1 c. shredded cheddar cheese
*optional, 1 c. cubed firm tofu

Preparation:
1. Preheat oven to 350 degrees.

2. Lightly spray a large casserole dish with nonstick cooking spray.

3. In a large bowl, whisk together the sour cream, chicken broth, and flour.

4. Stir in the potatoes, onion, ham, cheddar cheese, and tofu, if desired.

5. Spread the mixture evenly into the prepared casserole dish.

6. Bake for 45 minutes.

7. Remove from oven, and let sit for 15 minutes.

8. Serve warm.

Oatmeal Pancakes with Cinnamon Raisin Syrup

Syrup Ingredients:
2 c. water
½ c. sugar
2 tbsp. flour
2 tbsp. butter
¼ tsp. salt
1 tsp. vanilla extract
½ c. raisins
½ tsp. cinnamon

Oatmeal Pancakes Ingredients:
1 ½ c. quick oats
1 tbsp. flour
1 tbsp. brown sugar
1 tbsp. baking powder
2 tbsp. milled flaxseed
1 ¾ c. milk
1 tbsp. oil

Preparation:
1. To make the syrup, add the water to a saucepan, and bring it to a boil over medium-high heat.

2. Add the sugar, flour, butter, and salt, and cook until the mixture begins to thicken.

3. Remove the syrup from the heat, and stir in the vanilla extract, raisins, and cinnamon.

4. Set the syrup aside until the pancakes have been made.

5. To begin the pancakes, preheat a griddle to medium-high heat.

6. In a medium bowl, stir together the oats, flour, brown sugar, baking powder, flaxseed, milk, and oil until just combined.

7. Lightly spray the preheated griddle with nonstick cooking spray.

8. Drop the pancake batter by ¼ to ½ cupfuls, depending on the desired size of your pancakes, onto the griddle.

9. Cook the pancakes about 2 minutes, or until the edges begin to dry.

10. Flip the pancakes and cook another 2-3 minutes, or until lightly browned and firm.

11. Serve the pancakes warm with the cinnamon raisin syrup.

Orange Pineapple Yogurt Parfaits

Ingredients:
2 c. vanilla yogurt
1 c. crushed pineapple, drained
1 c. canned mandarin orange segments, drained
1 c. granola
1 c. whipped cream

Preparation:
1. Start with four clear 12-ounce milkshake glasses or tall glass dessert dishes.

2. Spoon ¼ cup of crushed pineapple into the bottom of each glass.

3. Top the pineapple with ¼ cup of yogurt.

4. Top the yogurt with ¼ cup of mandarin orange segments.

5. Top the mandarin orange segments with ¼ cup of yogurt.

6. Top the yogurt with ¼ cup of granola.

7. Top the granola with ¼ cup of whipped cream.

8. Serve immediately, or refrigerate and serve cold later.

Pancakes

Ingredients:
¾ c. whole wheat flour
2 tsp. baking powder
1 tbsp. sugar
¼ tsp. salt
2/3 c. milk
1/4 c. canola oil

Preparation:
1. Preheat a griddle to medium-high.

2. In a medium bowl, combine the flour, baking powder, sugar, and salt.

3. Stir in the milk and canola oil until just combined. Do not overmix.

4. Lightly grease the griddle just before cooking.

5. Drop batter by ¼ cupfuls onto the griddle, and cook until the edges are beginning to dry and bubbles begin to appear on top.

6. Flip the pancakes, and cook another 1-2 minutes.

7. Serve warm with butter, syrup, or jelly if desired.

Peach Coffee Cake

Ingredients:
¾ c. sugar
½ c. canola oil
½ c. sour cream
½ c. milk
2 tbsp. water
1 c. white flour
1 c. whole wheat flour
2 tbsp. milled flaxseed
1 tbsp. baking powder
½ tsp. baking soda
¼ tsp. salt
1 tsp. cinnamon
15 oz. can of peaches, drained and chopped
1/3 c. brown sugar

Preparation:
1. Preheat oven to 325 degrees F, and grease a 9x13-inch pan.

2. In a large bowl, mix together the sugar, oil, sour cream, milk, water, white flour, whole wheat flour, flaxseed, baking powder, baking soda, salt, cinnamon, and peaches until combined.

3. Pour the batter into the prepared pan.

4. Sprinkle the brown sugar evenly over the top.

5. Bake 45-50 minutes, or until a toothpick inserted in the center comes out clean.

6. Serve warm, at room temperature, or chilled.

Peanut Butter & Jelly Bars

Ingredients:
1 ½ c. whole wheat flour
¼ c. sugar
1 tsp. baking powder
1 tsp. ground flaxseed
1 tbsp. water
1/8 c. butter, softened
½ c. peanut butter, crunchy or creamy
½ c. grape jelly

Preparation:
1. Preheat oven to 400 degrees F.

2. Lightly grease an 8x8-inch pan with nonstick cooking spray.

3. In a medium bowl, cream together the butter, sugar, water, and peanut butter.

4. Add the flour, baking powder, and flaxseed, and stir until crumbly.

5. Press the crumbs evenly over the bottom of the prepared pan, reserving ½ cup of crumbs for later.

6. Spread the jelly evenly on top of the pressed crumbs.

7. Sprinkle the remaining ½ cup of crumbs on top of the jelly, and pat them down gently.

8. Bake for 15 minutes, or until browned.

9. Allow the bars to cool for at least 20 minutes before cutting them.

10. Serve warm or at room temperature with a glass of milk.

Peanut Butter & Jelly Pancakes

Ingredients:
1 c. flour
2 tsp. baking powder
1 tbsp. sugar
1 ½ c. milk
¼ c. canola oil
½ c. peanut butter
1 c. jelly

Preparation:
1. Preheat a griddle to medium heat.

2. In a medium bowl, combine the flour, baking powder, sugar, and salt.

3. Stir in the milk, canola oil, and peanut butter until just combined.

4. Lightly grease the griddle just before cooking.

5. Drop the batter by ¼ cupfuls onto the griddle, and cook until edges are beginning to dry and bubbles begin to appear on top.

6. Flip the pancakes, and cook another 1-2 minutes.

7. Serve warm with jelly.

Peanut Butter Banana Dogs

Ingredients:
4 bananas, peeled
4 whole wheat hot dog buns
4 tbsp. peanut butter
2 tsp. honey
*optional, raisins, walnuts, shredded coconut

Preparation:
1. Spread each hot dog bun with 1 tablespoon of peanut butter.

2. Place each banana in a prepared bun.

3. Drizzle each banana with ½ teaspoon of honey.

4. Top with raisins, walnuts, or coconut if desired.

5. Serve immediately.

Pineapple Upside Down Biscuits

Ingredients:
2 packages refrigerated biscuit dough, any brand
½ c. butter, melted
1 c. brown sugar
1 20 oz. can crushed pineapple, drained

Preparation:
1. Preheat oven to 350 degrees F, and grease a 9x13-inch pan.

2. In a medium bowl, combine the melted butter, brown sugar, and pineapple.

3. Spread the pineapple mixture evenly over the bottom of the prepared pan.

4. Separate the biscuits, and lay them evenly on top of the pineapple mixture in the pan

5. Bake for about 15 minutes, or until biscuits are lightly browned.

6. Remove the pan from the oven, and allow the biscuits to cool for 5-10 minutes before turning them upside down onto a serving platter.

7. Serve warm, with whipped cream if desired.

Pull Apart Sticky Bread

Ingredients:
1 loaf frozen bread dough, thawed
½ c. white sugar
¾ c. brown sugar
1 tbsp. cinnamon
1/2 c. butter
½ c. chopped walnuts
½ c. raisins
½ c. shredded coconut

Preparation:
1. Allow the bread dough to rise as directed on the package.

2. Preheat oven to 350 degrees F, and grease a bundt pan.

3. In a large bowl, combine the white sugar, cinnamon, walnuts, raisins, and coconut.

4. Cut or tear the bread dough into 1-inch pieces.

5. Add the bread dough pieces to the bowl containing the white sugar mixture, and stir until coated.

5. Pour the contents of the bowl into the prepared bundt pan, and arrange so it's evenly distributed.

6. In a saucepan on the stove, melt the butter over medium heat, and stir in the brown sugar.

7. Bring the butter mixture to a boil, then remove it from the heat, and pour it over the bread dough in the bundt pan.

8. Allow to rise for 40-45 minutes.

9. Bake for 20 minutes or until browned.

8. Let the bread cool in the pan for about 10 minutes, then turn it out onto a serving plate.

10. Serve warm or at room temperature.

Pumpkin Muffins

Ingredients:
1 c. canned pumpkin
1 c. vanilla yogurt
1 tbsp. canola oil
3 tbsp. water
2 tsp. baking soda
1 tsp. cinnamon
1/8 tsp. nutmeg
½ tsp. ginger
1 tbsp. ground flaxseed
1 c. light brown sugar
¼ c. sugar
1/8 tsp. salt
2 ½ c. whole wheat flour
*optional, ½ c. ground walnuts

Preparation:
1. Preheat oven to 350 degrees F.

2. Lightly grease 18 muffin cups with nonstick cooking spray.

3. In a medium bowl, combine the pumpkin, yogurt, oil, water, soda, cinnamon, nutmeg, ginger, flaxseed, brown sugar, sugar, and salt.

4. Add the flour, and walnuts if desired, and stir until just combined. Don't overmix the batter.

5. Divide the batter evenly between the 18 muffin cups.

6. Bake on the center oven rack for 20 minutes or until the tops spring back when gently pressed.

7. Allow the muffins to cool before removing them from the cups.

8. Serve warm or at room temperature.

Rice Pudding

Ingredients:
2 c. cooked brown rice (white rice may be substituted)
4 c. milk
1 c. sugar
1 tsp. cinnamon
1/8 tsp. nutmeg
1 tsp. vanilla extract
½ c. raisins
3/8 c. cornstarch
¼ c. water

Preparation:
1. In a small bowl, whisk together the cornstarch and water.

2. In a large saucepan on the stove, bring the cooked rice, milk, sugar, cinnamon, nutmeg, vanilla extract, raisins, and cornstarch mixture to a full boil over medium-high heat, stirring constantly.

3. Boil for 1 minute, while still stirring constantly.

4. Turn off the heat, and allow the pudding to sit for 10-15 minutes to thicken.

5. Serve warm.

Sausage & Potato Balls

Ingredients:
1 lb. loose pork sausage
¼ tsp. onion salt
½ c. shredded cheddar cheese
¼ c. diced onion
¼ c. diced green pepper
½ c. peeled, shredded potato
½ c. baking mix (any brand)

Preparation:
1. Preheat oven to 350 degrees F.

2. Lightly grease a baking sheet with nonstick cooking spray.

3. In a medium bowl, combine the sausage, salt, cheddar cheese, onion, pepper, and potato.

4. Add baking mix, and mix together by hand.

5. Shape the sausage mixture into 1-inch balls, and place them on the prepared cookie sheet.

6. Bake until they reach 170 degrees (for about 20 minutes or until brown).

7. Serve warm.

Sausage Breakfast Burritos

Ingredients:
1 lb. loose pork sausage
½ c. diced onion
½ c. diced green pepper
1 c. peeled, diced potato
1 c. shredded cheddar cheese
*optional, 1 c. cubed firm tofu
4-6 flour tortillas

Preparation:
1. Add sausage, onion, green pepper, and potato to a large skillet, and cook over medium heat until sausage is browned (about 10 minutes), stirring occasionally to break the sausage apart.

2. Drain the grease, and add the tofu, if desired.

3. Sprinkle the cheddar cheese on top, and allow it to melt.

4. Divide the sausage mixture evenly between the flour tortillas.

5. Roll the tortilla shells to form burritos, and secure them each with a toothpick, if desired.

7. Serve warm.

Sausage Gravy over Drop Biscuits

Drop Biscuit Ingredients:
1 ½ c. flour
1 tsp. sugar
1 tbsp. baking powder
¾ c. milk

Sausage Gravy Ingredients:
1 lb. loose breakfast sausage
3 c. milk
¼ c. flour
½ tsp. salt
½ tsp. onion powder
1 tsp. ground black or white pepper

Preparation:
1. Preheat oven to 350 degrees F, and lightly grease a baking sheet with nonstick cooking spray.

2. In a medium bowl, mix together the flour, sugar, baking powder, and milk.

3. Drop the biscuit dough by heaping tablespoonfuls onto the prepared baking sheet.

4. Bake 12-15 minutes or until browned on bottom.

5. While the biscuits are baking, cook the sausage in a large skillet on the stove over medium heat for about 8 minutes, or until cooked through, stirring occasionally to break it apart.

6. When the sausage is cooked, drain the grease, and return the pan to the heat.

7. Stir in the milk, flour, salt, onion powder, and ground pepper, and bring to a boil, stirring occasionally.

8. Reduce heat, and simmer 5 minutes, or until it begins to thicken, stirring occasionally.

9. Remove from heat and let sit for 5 minutes to finish thickening.

10. Serve the sausage gravy warm over the biscuits.

Sausage Pinwheels

Ingredients:
1 loaf frozen bread dough, thawed
½ lb. loose pork sausage
¼ c. diced onion
½ c. cottage cheese

Preparation:
1. Preheat oven to 350 degrees F.

2. Lightly grease a large baking sheet with nonstick cooking spray, or line the baking sheet with parchment paper.

3. In a skillet on the stove, cook the sausage and onion over medium heat for about 8 minutes, stirring occasionally to break apart the sausage, until cooked through.

4. Remove the sausage from the heat, drain the grease, stir in the cottage cheese, and set aside.

5. Roll the bread dough to a rectangle about ¼ inch thick.

6. Spread the sausage mixture evenly over the bread dough.

7. Roll the bread dough up jelly roll style.

8. Slice the dough into 1-inch thick slices.

9. Place the slices swirl side up on the prepared pan.

10. Bake about 30 minutes, or until beginning to lightly brown.

11. Serve warm.

Steak & Potato Breakfast Burritos

Ingredients:
1 lb. steak (any cut will work) cubed or sliced into strips
½ c. diced onion
1 c. peeled, diced potato
1 c. shredded mozzarella cheese
*optional, 1 c. cubed firm tofu
1 c. salsa
4-6 flour tortillas

Preparation:
1. Grease a large skillet.

2. Add steak, onion, and potato to the skillet, and cook over medium heat until steak is browned and no longer pink inside (about 6-8 minutes), stirring occasionally to cook steak on all sides.

3. Add the tofu, if desired.

4. Sprinkle the mozzarella cheese on top, and allow it to melt.

5. Divide the steak mixture evenly between the flour tortillas.

6. Top each burrito with an equal amount of salsa.

7. Roll the tortilla shells to form burritos, and secure them each with a toothpick, if desired.

8. Serve warm.

Strawberry Banana Smoothies

Ingredients:
2 medium bananas
1 c. strawberry yogurt
1 tbsp. honey
1 c. milk or soy milk
4 ice cubes

Preparation:
1. Place all ingredients in a blender.

2. Blend until smooth.

3. Serve immediately.

*Note: Since the sizes of bananas vary, the consistency of the smoothies may vary also. If the smoothies are too thick, add more milk as needed, and blend until desired consistency is reached. If the smoothies are too thin, add another banana, and blend to desired consistency.

Sweet Buttery Corn Grits

Ingredients:
1 ½ c. water
1/8 tsp. salt
½ c. corn grits
¼ c. butter
¼ c. honey

Preparation:
1. In a saucepan on the stove, bring the water to a boil.

2. Stir in the salt and corn grits, and reduce heat to medium-low.

3. Cook for 5 minutes, stirring occasionally.

4. Remove from heat, and stir in butter and honey.

5. Cover the grits, and let them stand for about 3-5 minutes, and they will thicken slightly

6. Serve warm.

Sweet Cornbread Breakfast Muffins

Ingredients:
1 c. cornmeal
1 c. flour
1 tbsp. baking powder
1 tsp. baking soda
¾ c. buttermilk
1/3 c. honey
2 tbsp. canola oil
1 c. shredded cheddar cheese
1 c. cooked, diced ham or 1/3 c. crumbled bacon
*optional, ¼ c. diced jalapeno peppers or sweet peppers

Preparation:
1. Preheat oven to 375 degrees F, and grease 18 muffin cups.

2. In a large bowl, combine the cornmeal, flour, baking powder, and baking soda.

3. Stir in the buttermilk, honey, and canola oil.

4. Gently fold in the shredded cheddar cheese, ham or bacon, and peppers if desired.

5. Distribute the batter evenly among the 18 prepared muffin cups.

6. Bake 20-25 minutes, or until golden brown.

7. Remove the muffins from the oven, and let them sit for 5-10 minutes before removing them from the muffin cups.

8. Serve warm.

Sweet Potato Biscuits

Ingredients:
2 c. whole wheat flour
1 tbsp. baking powder
1 tsp. cinnamon
¼ c. butter
¾ c. milk
½ c. cooked, mashed sweet potatoes

Preparation:
1. Preheat oven to 450 degrees F.

2. In a medium bowl, combine the flour, baking powder, and cinnamon.

3. Cut the butter into the dry ingredients with a pastry mixer, forks, or knives.

4. Add the milk and sweet potatoes, and mix with a fork until a ball forms.

5. Turn dough onto a lightly floured surface, and knead for 1 minute.

6. Roll the dough out to a ½-inch thickness

7. Slice the dough into 12 pieces with a knife, or cut out desired shapes with a cookie cutter.

8. Place the biscuits on an ungreased cookie sheet, and bake for 10-12 minutes.

9. Serve warm or at room temperature, with butter if desired.

Triple Apple Muffins

Ingredients:
1 ½ c. whole wheat flour
½ c. sugar
2 tsp. baking powder
½ tsp. salt
1 tbsp. ground flaxseed
3 tbsp. water
½ c. applesauce
1 c. peeled, cored, grated apple
1 c. apple butter

Preparation:
1. Preheat oven to 400 degrees F.

2. Lightly grease 12 muffin cups with nonstick cooking spray.

3. In a medium bowl, combine the water, applesauce, sugar, baking powder, ground flaxseed, grated apple, and salt.

4. Add the flour and stir until just combined. Don't overmix the batter.

5. Divide the batter evenly between the 12 muffin cups.

6. Top each muffin with an equal amount of apple butter.

7. Bake on the center oven rack for 20-25 minutes or until lightly browned.

8. Allow the muffins to cool before removing them from the cups.

9. Serve warm or at room temperature.

Vegetarian Tofu Scramble

Ingredients:
1 tbsp. butter
½ c. chopped onion
½ c. chopped green pepper
½ c. sliced mushrooms
½ c. chopped tomato
2 c. cubed extra firm tofu
½ tsp. salt
½ tsp. ground black pepper or lemon pepper seasoning

Preparation:
1. In a large skillet on the stove, melt the butter over medium heat.

2. Add the onion and green pepper, and sauté for 3 minutes, stirring occasionally.

3. Stir in the mushrooms and tomato, and cook another 3 minutes.

4. Remove from heat and stir in the tofu, salt, and pepper.

5. Let the scramble sit for 3 minutes to warm the tofu.

6. Serve warm.

Waffles

Ingredients:
1 c. whole wheat flour
1 tbsp. baking powder
1 tbsp. sugar
½ tsp. salt
1 tsp. milled flaxseed
2 tsp. vanilla extract
¾ c. milk
¼ c. canola oil

Preparation:
1. Preheat waffle iron.

2. In a medium bowl, combine the flour, baking powder, sugar, salt, and flaxseed.

3. Stir in the vanilla extract, milk, and canola oil.

4. Lightly spray the waffle iron with nonstick cooking spray.

5. Pour the batter by 1/3 cupfuls into the waffle iron, and close the lid.

6. Cook 2-3 minutes or until the amount of steam emitted by the waffle iron decreases.

7. Remove the waffles from the waffle iron, and serve warm with butter and syrup if desired.

Makes 5-6 four-inch square waffles.

Walnut Spice Waffles

Ingredients:
1 c. whole wheat flour
1 tbsp. baking powder
1 tbsp. sugar
½ tsp. salt
1 tsp. milled flaxseed
1/8 tsp. nutmeg
1 tsp. cinnamon
¼ c. ground walnuts
¾ c. milk
¼ c. canola oil

Preparation:
1. Preheat waffle iron.

2. In a medium bowl, combine the flour, baking powder, sugar, salt, flaxseed, nutmeg, cinnamon, and walnuts.

3. Stir in the milk and canola oil.

4. Lightly spray the waffle iron with nonstick cooking spray.

5. Pour the batter by 1/3 cupfuls into the waffle iron, and close the lid.

6. Cook 2-3 minutes or until the amount of steam emitted by the waffle iron decreases.

7. Remove the waffles from the waffle iron, and serve warm with butter and syrup if desired.

Makes 5-6 four-inch square waffles.

Notes:

www.RandiLynnMillward.com